I'm good at

Helping

Eileen Day

www.raintreepublishers.co.uk
Visit our website to find out more information about Raintree books.

To order:
☎ Phone 44 (0) 1865 888112
📠 Send a fax to 44 (0) 1865 314091
💻 Visit the Heinemann Bookshop at www.raintreepublishers.co.uk to browse our catalogue and order online.

GLOUCESTERSHIRE COUNTY LIBRARY	
9929724125	
PETERS	07-Feb-06
158.1	£5.25

First published in Great Britain by Raintree, Halley Court, Jordan Hill, Oxford OX2 8EJ, part of Harcourt Education.
Raintree is a registered trademark of Harcourt Education Ltd.

© Harcourt Education Ltd 2003
First published in paperback in 2004
The moral right of the proprietor has been asserted.

All rights reserved. No part of this publication may be reproduced, stored in a retrieval system, or transmitted in any form or by any means, electronic, mechanical, photocopying, recording, or otherwise, without either the prior written permission of the publishers or a licence permitting restricted copying in the United Kingdom issued by the Copyright Licensing Agency Ltd, 90 Tottenham Court Road, London W1T 4LP (www.cla.co.uk).

Editorial: Nick Hunter and Diyan Leake
Design: Michelle Lisseter
Picture Research: Alan Gottlieb and Amor Montes de Oca
Production: Lorraine Hicks

Originated by Dot Gradations
Printed and bound in China by South China Printing Company

ISBN 1 844 21502 4 (hardback)
07 06 05 04 03
10 9 8 7 6 5 4 3 2 1

ISBN 1 844 21509 1 (paperback)
08 07 06 05 04
10 9 8 7 6 5 4 3 2 1

British Library Cataloguing in Publication Data
Day, Eileen
Helping. – (I'm good at)
158.3
A full catalogue record for this book is available from the British Library.

Acknowledgements
The publishers would like to thank the following for permission to reproduce photographs: Bob Daemmrich Photo, Inc., **17**; Corbis/Ariel Skelley, **11**, **21**; Corbis/Craig Hammell, **14**, **21**; Corbis/Norbert Schafer, **5**, **7**, **21**; FLPA/Sunset, **12**; Getty Images/Digital Vision, **20**; Getty Images/EyeWire, **10**, **23**; Getty Images/Taxi, **9**; Heinemann Library/Robert Lifson, **22**, **24**; John Walmsley, **4**; Mrs. Kevin Scheibel Photography, **16**; PhotoDisc, **6**, **18**, **23**; Photo Edit/David Young-Wolff, **13**, **21**; PhotoEdit/Richard Hutchings, **19**; Pictor International, **15**; Rex Features/ nils Jorgensen, **23**; Stock Boston/Lawrence Migdale, **8**; Trevor Clifford, **23**.

Cover photograph reproduced with permission of Corbis/Michael Pole.

Every effort has been made to contact copyright holders of any material reproduced in this book. Any omissions will be rectified in subsequent printings if notice is given to the publishers.

Some words are shown in bold, **like this**. They are explained in the glossary on page 23.

Contents

What is helping?................. 4

How can I help at home? 6

How can I help with the shopping? .. 8

How can I help my brother? 10

How can I help outside? 12

How can I help in my community? ... 14

How can I help my neighbour? 16

How can I help at school? 18

How do I feel when I help? 20

Quiz 22

Glossary 23

Index 24

Answer to quiz................ 24

What is helping?

Helping is doing something for someone else.

There are helpers in your **community**.

You can help at home.

You can help in your community, too.

How can I help at home?

You can help Mum make dinner.

You can help make a **pizza**.

Later, you can help clean the kitchen.

You can help with the washing-up.

How can I help with the shopping?

You go to the shops to buy food.

You can put fruit in a bag.

You can help Mum at the **supermarket**.

You can put food in the trolley.

How can I help my brother?

At the seaside, you can help your brother build a **sandcastle**.

You can put sand in a bucket.

At home, you can help your brother give the dog a bath.

You can spray water on the dog.

How can I help outside?

You can help in the **garden**.

You can grow flowers and vegetables.

First, you dig a hole.

Then, you put in a seed.

How can I help in my community?

You can help keep the park clean.

You can put rubbish in the bin.

You can sweep the pavement.

You can rake up autumn leaves.

How can I help my neighbour?

Your neighbour lives in the house next door.

You can take her newspaper to her.

You can take her dog for a walk.

It is fun to help your neighbour.

How can I help at school?

You can help your teacher.

You can tell her the date.

You can help look after the class pet.

You can give it food to eat.

How do I feel when I help?

Helping makes you feel happy.

It makes other people happy, too.

You can help every day.

When you help it makes you smile!

21

Quiz

How can you help here?

Look for the answer on page 24.

Glossary

community
area around where you live

garden
land around a house where there can be grass, plants and trees

pizza
round, flat dough base covered in tomatoes, cheese and other toppings, then baked

sandcastle
shapes made by filling a bucket with sand and then turning it upside-down

supermarket
large shop that sells food, things for the home, and sometimes clothes

Index

community   4, 5, 14–15, 23

feelings   20–21

flowers   12

fruit   8

garden   12, 23

neighbour   16, 17

outside   12

park   14

pizza   6, 23

rake   15

sand   10

sandcastle   10, 23

school   18

supermarket   9, 23

vegetables   12

Answer to quiz on page 22
You can put rubbish in the bin.